A COLLECTION OF
POETRY & PROSE

JAGGED
LITTLE PIECES

BY KELLIE ELMORE

Winter Goose
Publishing

Winter Goose Publishing
2701 Del Paso Road, 130-92
Sacramento, CA 95835

www.wintergoosepublishing.com
Contact Information: info@wintergoosepublishing.com

Jagged Little Pieces

COPYRIGHT © 2013 by Kellie Elmore

First Edition, March 2013

Cover Art by Winter Goose Publishing
Photograph by Kellie Elmore
Typeset by Michelle Lovi

ISBN: 978-0-9889049-6-5

Published in the United States of America

FOR MYSELF; HERE'S TO HEALING

Who are you? they ask of me
and my tongue falls numb
the answer they seek
is hidden

A mother, a child
a wife
a writer of things
I think to be me

Not what but who
they inquire once more
and I look at the ceiling

Dreamer; passionate,
shy, hopeful,
hopeless

I am not who I was
and not who I'll be
Who am I? I ask of me

"I don't want someone to believe my lies; I need someone to accept my truths."

—*Kellie Elmore*

INTRODUCTION

I see the world from this chair and feel it beneath my fingertips as I peck. Sirens outside my window and howling dogs of the neighborhood are the only things that remind me I'm not in a perfect place as I make believe I am . . . and I peck some more.

Pauses come and go like halting trains carrying thoughts and ideas, and I am in a broken car watching it sit on the tracks, waiting; we're all just waiting. And I think of Charles, his days of empty pockets and how he died of Leukemia . . . and I pull another drag.

Not long before they come sneaking in, those demons. And I find myself reaching for the scars, picking scabs from old wounds; unforgettable and ominous pieces of me, reuniting myself with the pain, much like an old friend. And I have to go back there and free them, in just a few lines to ease the ache and then I can try once more to see beauty in the world without tears blurring the view.

I picture the daffodils and try to imagine their dance like William did in moods of melancholy and sometimes, sometimes they do sway my wandering mind to happiness, though, only for a time.

And after the raging of words, when it all becomes just too much, the pecking stops.

CHAPTERS

Jagged Little Pieces (pieces of depression)

Roaming Between Shores (pieces of hope)

IT'S ALWAYS RAINING
~PIECES OF DEATH~

THERE'S A REASON

There's a reason for the sunset
and winter and death
a reason for the last page
of every story told
of love and life
and in growing old
there's a reason
I keep telling myself
there's a reason

IT'S ALWAYS RAINING

Imagine for a moment
the first person that comes to mind
when I say you love them.

This person would never hurt you.
That someone
you can always count on.

Now,
that person, or those people
who crossed your mind,
who warmed your heart,
they just died. Gone. Poof.

And you can't think, you can't
bring to mind anyone else
that you could turn to and
all of your shoulders are gone.

And now,
now you feel it
that loneliness
it's cold, you're lost
and it's always raining.

This
is the decline
of me,
and the losses,
and the pain,

and the tears I fight daily,
all together in a mind whirl
downward
that has been falling so far
and for so long that
my heart has moved past the shock
and just went to sleep
waiting for someone,
or something,
to pound on my chest
to wake me.

SINGING MYSELF TO WAKE

If I told you; reverie
clings to me like shadows
cast from trees, alone
in the middle of
summer-singed fields
that call to me,
remember,
as I pass by while
out driving because
I'm sad again. And the
murmuring road seems to
soothe the ache,

and the smoke that creeps off
the tip of my cigarette and
into the dim,
scattered strands of light
leaking off the moon, in
through clefts in the curtains,
is much like my spirit
trying to escape the burn
of yesterday's presence,

that my eyes sting
in grievous winds of detriment,
hiding them from me,
pushing me toward catatonia and
I fight anchored lids
from falling stuporous
would you understand

these words; these frozen,
metaphoric lullabies that
I sing myself to wake, to
induce serenity, to mute death,
or would it even matter,

would you, could you understand?

DEAR DEATH

I think about you a lot more than I should. You have stolen so many pieces of my heart away and left me in perpetual mourning. You linger in the front lobe of my brain, and every turn I near, there you are. You haunt me and I cannot live for the needle of worry you have straight-lined into my veins.

I remember when you first came. It was my uncle Lester, and I stood about three feet tall and listened to firing guns as they lowered him into the ground. I felt you standing behind me and you were so cold. I didn't give you any tears that day. You were a stranger, odd and distant.

You came back for my uncle Lowell, and then two of my grandpa's and I got to know you a little better and tears came, but they remained few until . . .

You came back like a lion's roar, rumbling my whole existence, demanding I take notice of you and I did. You took her. My sweet grandma, the one who held me all the times you came before. Now, there I was, holding her hand while you crept into the room and began to slowly pull her from my grip. It was then I realized, you were never going to leave me alone, and every time you returned you would make sure it hurt a little more, and you have done so accordingly.

You came and stole Uncle Greg while he slept. Why? Why couldn't you just let us say goodbye? You didn't even call ahead this time! I hate you for that; your cruelty is unforgiving and now, just before Christmas, when children are supposed to be happy and grandkids are wishing for snow, you come in like a blizzard and snatch him away, my father, their granddad, during what should be the merriest of seasons, and forever taint this time of year for everyone who loved him. Why must you be so cold?

I know now, you are inevitable. I know that I will cry again. I know that you will one day come for me, too, and this is all that I think of every day, every minute, every second. I constantly await your return when I want to cast you like a stone into the deep, but . . .

I am the one drowning instead.

FREEZING PAIN

he comes toward me in a snowstorm
and Itzhak's violin weeps
in dark, thick, heavy wool
iris of hypnotic violet, peering
from white-slit sheets of
horizontal paper-cuts; invisible,
yet irrefutably present, and
I sizzle in his gaze, dying with
each breath he fills into me, like
a dagger piercing my lung, and I am
left breathless.

MOVE AGAIN

The refrigerator hums
and I hear cars wisp by outside.
Where are they going?
Who are they with?
I consider turning the radio on,
but it might make me think of you.

The train blows
just when I was forgetting—
forgetting that I am here alone—
and I wonder if those cars
got held up by its passing
just as I have, yours.

The only difference is,
they will soon move again.

GHOSTS AT THE KITCHEN DOOR

I swear I heard you in the kitchen
yelling out hey
when you came in through the back door.

Hey.

I looked
and for a split second
I saw you, too.

But, of course, you weren't there
because you're dead.

And here I am
writing about you again.

JUST FOR ME

I used to close my eyes
and imagine them near;
so close I could smell them.
I'd imagine them whispering;
comforting words in my ear
telling me how beautiful
that place is and
how happy they are now,
and I would reach out
to touch them.
Then, something shook me,
snapped its fingers and
made me realize,
they're not here,
they're not trying to
tell me anything,
because
if that place
is so wonderful
why would they bother
coming back here
just for me?

NOVEMBER

It's November now
and I still wear these old flip-flops.
It reminds me of you
and how you went barefoot year round
not caring what anyone thought.
I wish I could be more like you.

The football game is on the radio,
your favorite team; play by play, I listen
driving around this town
littered with politician signs
and piles of leaves on roadsides.
Cold things,
that's what they remind me of.

I miss your face;
that big, bright smile,
you always had it, in any weather.
It's hard for me to find one
these days—
these cold, November days—
except when I think of you.

And they all keep saying,
he loved this time of year.

DECEMBER

Loneliness lingers on a wisp
of peppermint in December air,
clinging to an old sweater
I still see in photographs.
Grief consumes the joy,
stealing the twinkle from
holiday lights and sets instead
a teardrop in my eye, and
I wrap my arms around myself
because they can no more
and no one else will.

THE HAZE OF KNOWING

Somewhere within the light resting of my
fingertips on his back and stitched eyes
peeling away to look upon the window where
the bird song trickles in—mind wandering;
a dusty suitcase beckons my memory through
a muffled wisp between the barbed thorn branch
and pecking death. In every man's mirror—
staring into the eyes of this being I know
so well, and yet, I know nothing—while
familiar, the mystery lingers back at me like a
glaring stranger in the fog, moving closer and
closer and closer. The haze gives
blur to the form of their face but, I know,
and I close my eyes and feel its clarity as it
presents behind closed eyelids and dreamscapes;
déjà vu flickers, catching like a card in
bicycle spokes, frame by frame of
yesterday and tomorrow. And who is he coming for
today, as faces flash in grainy pictures in the
forefront of my mind and in the distortion and
static of the airwaves on the radio, echoing voices
that traveled another road? No more, no more, no more.
Another piece falls from a generation's puzzle that
will be extinct in less than a hundred years.

WHERE MANY TEARS HAVE FALLEN

We stood weeping
in a field of sorrow
surrounded by stone faces
we mourned before.
In that same place
again
we gathered,
where many tears have
already fallen.
And we looked upon them
as the dirt fell
and I wondered
who of us
would follow and
who would remain weeping
in this field of sorrow
beside his stone face
where many tears
have already fallen

FOR STEVE

LIVE OR DIE

Into its beyond all will go
and through it some shall pass
inside holds secrets never broken
but by few who fought back
and within its shaded void
we all shall one day lie
naught its shadow will one avoid
live or die
live or die

BETWEEN DUSK AND DAYBREAK

In a lurking fog howls the ghost of sadness,
its hands clenching neck, unable to swallow
tears. Black and white bleed together, graying
and erasing the horizon, creeping down on you
like a spider on a silken strand, in beautiful
silence; dropping softly, slowly, and now
you see life only from the corner of your eye.

And it first grazes your skin—paranoia,
taunting—and then, it bites; sharp and
penetrating before paralyzing, then glazed,
random, worrisome, mind chaos, pulling
like quicksand swallowing every breath
as you watch life, and movement in
hazy motion, and you continue searching for
one still moment to place your foot on,
but clock's spinning seconds leaves time
stranded at midnight, between dusk and
daybreak—
click . . .

click . . .

click . . .
and eyes fixed on wounds burn,
yet seep no more.

UNCLE'S GHOST

A hymn I knew well came through the radio; a
crescendo, gripping me like an old friend saying
a goodbye I had heard so many times before;
standing graveside, beside caskets, pushing up
sorrow from my heart to spill from my eyes.
He sat beside me, watching intently as
my face formed sad, weeping expressions
and my mouth, between sobs, trying to sing,
but only able to gather a word or two.
I seemed to float in and out of memories,
lost in thoughts of moments I wished I had
just held a little closer. Squandered time and
what-ifs that haunt me. Those words,
I think I need to rest for a while
repeated over and over in my mind,
and I tried to focus on the road ahead,
catching myself drifting into the blue of the sky
making pictures of clouds to distract from the hurt,
unable to wipe the tears fast enough
before my face would be drowned again.
His hand reached slowly towards me,
he wanted to wipe away my pain,
whispering a reminder,
do not mourn, the spirit never dies.
He touched my cheek, I felt it,
a rushing peace—exhaling a sigh of
relief that seemed to release the pressure
off my heavy, aching chest and
I knew he was with me as I
looked into the empty passenger seat
and whispered back, *I miss you.*

REMEMBER ME DUST

they come visit me from time to time
in early spring as ghosts who creep
and sprinkle the earth
with remember me dust
and the flowers bloom; orange lilies
she planted beside the house
or the pear tree he placed in the front yard
and sometimes I smell them
just a subtle whiff
a passerby in the breeze
her lotion
his cologne
another reminder that they were here again
or to tell me that they were never really gone

LIKE THE DYING

I wish I could rest for a while;
I sleep but it brings no ease.
My head keeps running
like a stream from a broken faucet,
and it won't turn off.

I recount so many yesterdays, haunted
by the sadness of their passing,
swelling and wallowing in remorse for
things that will never return,
things I can never make right,
things I wish I could do over again.
And I remind myself of the dying
trying to fix corridors of the past
before the wrecking ball falls.

Then, I remember,
I am dying,
but aren't we all?

BENEATH SIX FEET OF FORGOTTEN

Faces diminish into scattered pixels,
voices silence like a song's faded ending,
becoming a memory,
lost somewhere in life's distractions.

Belonging to souls once bonded,
winter weakens the embrace
that once seemed unbreakable,
chilling bones and recollection
now, as if it had never existed.

How do we forget being shattered?

How do we forget being broken; bent in
agony, sending a goodbye into forever,
promising to hold close to roots
that are now wilted faces
hidden beneath six feet of forgotten.

CROSSING OVER

I have often wondered about death,
when it happens, when you go.
And I imagine it as a train,
a big, loud, roaring, screeching
fiery engine of steel and smoke,
barreling towards railroad crossings,
daring someone to try and cheat him,
to try and just *slip* past
right before the gates come down.
And for those that fail, those that
hesitated just a second too long
and were swallowed by him,
did they hear his scream
and do they remember their own,
or do they just simply awake
on the other side of the tracks,
watching him pass in the rearview,
never even knowing they are dead—
travelling on and on unaware and
the world around them is fiction,
made up of memories of the familiar,
and could it be,
could this be hell?
A repeated reality of all our sufferings
infinitely searching for Heaven
or
do we just die there
smeared across the tracks of our life,
forgotten?

IMAGINING DEATH

Last night, I imagined you not being here,
not gone like to work or in the woods hunting,
knowing that you will call me on your way home,
but I imagined you dead.

I thought of coming home to an empty house
and curling up in our unmade bed, sobbing,
endlessly sobbing,
gripping your lumpy pillow trying to
just breathe you inside of me,
replaying every little moment with you,
all the happy ones I know you would remember too.
Over and over and over and over again,
wanting desperately to hear your voice say
Hey, baby
and wanting to wrap my arms around you and
smell your dirty, oil-stained work shirt I hate so much.
And wanting to bring you a dinner plate
like I do when I complain how tired I am, too.
I imagined you dead and all of those things made me sad,
and I thought of how happy I would be to do them again,
and when the headlights hit the bedroom window
when you came home from work.
I imagined those things and I jumped up,
fixed your dinner plate,
got the washer ready for your dirty old shirt
and I curled up beside you in our unmade bed,
smiling as you try fluffing your lumpy pillow
and so very happy you're here.

ONE LAST PETAL

voices say
it's time to gather rosebuds
whispering
from invisible places
I cover my ears
and eyes
I am not ready yet, I say
go away
go away
go away
I whisper back
and for a time
I ignore their presence
as they stand behind cloaks
hands out
reaching for my last petal
and they keep returning
reminding me
they can't stay away forever

FUNERALS WITH TREES

Comfort sits on my shoulder
whispering promises it cannot keep,
and I'm a fool for believing.

Early morning,
I exit the house through the back door
and sit on the cold stoop with swollen eyes
that won't dry, because it's happened again,
because I'll never sing another lullaby.

And I ask again,
why, why, why
while the trees stand still
staring at me like they know,
their hats off and hanging heads.

While faith is dying, stabbed again
by that lying bitch named hope,
and I mourn the maybes of pinks and blues
fighting not as she falters before me,
I cannot save her again,
I don't want to.

I'm tired
of making the trees sad.

LOVING THE DEAD

I love you.
You knew that and
maybe you still do, but
you're gone now and
it's all I have left . . .

to love you.

It's a burden,
carrying you in my mind.
I never knew that
ghosts could be so heavy,
and I have to let go now.

TANGLED WEBS
~PIECES OF LOVE~

MORPHINE KISSES

I search for a hand
to mend my perforated heart,
blown open by a bullet
welded by lies.

A tender hand to hold steady,
a thread of truth on an honest
needle to re-stitch my
wound of discernment.

A conferral hand to dose me
with morphine kisses
to remedy the pain of
my suicidal soul.

A kind hand,
a warm hand,
a hand to hurt me no more.

SWEET AND SOUR

Wanton;
like a kiss that never meets
between lips only a breath apart,
longing, desperately for one taste
of its sweet and tender truth; love,
and the beautiful ideas of and
proof of its existence, tainted not
by a sour tongue.

HATE LOVE

It does conquer all:
love.
With its hard hand
slapped against your face
or gripped around your heart,
it does indeed conquer.

I feel it unimaginable to place
love and hate in the same sentence
like
I hate love,
but they belong together
in their beautifully, bittersweet agony;
miserably together.

And yet,
we can't seem to get enough,
so we walk around with
a shovel over our shoulder,
eager to dig our own graves.

Because it will always kill us
somehow.

TANGLED WEBS

You know you shouldn't
but you swallow them anyway,
chased with a strong shot of
your own bullshit justification,
all to satisfy the beast of need
and it's hunger for affection
so you manipulate his words,
twisting them and stringing them,
winding them just so,
until they begin to whisper
what it is you need to hear;
what you want him to say
but he never will,
and in the end, you question
who was the bigger liar.

SLAVE

Every thought
orbits him—
gripped inside his
unrelenting gravity;
helpless.
He reigns over my
very being,
footsteps determined by
his lead,
words spoken to
please.
A slave, am I,
willingly unwilling
to breathe on my own.
Content in chains
of this need.

THE POSTURE OF A BROKEN BACKBONE

farewell brushed my limbs
in spotted chills, prickling hair;
settled on a breeze from his cold
and fruitless breath, to move
away from my body, kneeling
not in worship as before but
in grievous bends on splintered,
broken ground, ripping my flesh,
spilling salt and blood from
eyes and a faltering heart,
begging for merciful words
begging for pieces of lies
to touch honesty,
to repair the cracked bone of
my wretched, crippled back
that betrayed me and left me
fragile and broken

NO FERRYMAN

in the dusty corners of my mind
rests your name
my lips stitched closed to keep you
from falling, to keep me from falling
buried there in the darkness of
faded summers and torn pixels from
photographic memories ripped apart
and I keep you locked there in silence
behind thoughts that wonder if what he says
is true—comparisons to lies once told
believed and swallowed like a pill to
keep me happy for a while and now
he pays your debt
as I squeeze your lies from him
waiting for signs, waiting for clues
to warn me before I am played a fool
again but you are the one who owes me
two coins for my eyes, for
leaving me abandoned on a dock of
questioning and paranoia with
no ferryman in sight to cross me over

STAGNANT INTENTIONS

I know that look,
when you whisper with your eyes,
reminding me of
our little secret.
I watch in angst. You kiss her and look my way
It's not her I want,
speaks from your eyes,
or maybe,
it's just another lie I tell myself.

My hands are clammy.
The deafening thump in my chest,
faster and faster.
Holding my breath,
I think I could vomit just watching,
but the lump in my throat won't let me.

Tripping over words
and my own feet,
shaking and stumbling,
trying to run,
slowed by a million shallow breaths
through deep pools of humiliation.

Then, I cry alone and
drown in stagnant intentions.

You call with no apologies, but I hear them;
Another lie but to myself.
I am better. I forget. And it begins again—
shallow breaths and thumping chest.

SPINNING BOTTLES

Sultry like August; burning
inside these sheets, lying
tangible flesh,
but that's all that is here,
led in by spinning bottles—
empty.

Give me something else
besides smoke rings on a burning finger.
I'm not asking you to leave
while the cold floor gives you reasons
to put on your shoes
and walk out before it's time
to turn off the porch light.

PICK ME

Maybe, if I die
I will get to come back as a flower,
and people will write poems;
verses of my beauty,
and maybe
they will sing love songs
from drunken lips,
intoxicated on my fragrance.
Maybe
I shall become a perennial
to place in their bed
for more than just a season,
and I will be gazed upon
as they paint me onto canvas,
and maybe,
just maybe,
someone will finally
pick me.

IN THE SILENCE OF MAKE BELIEVE

They came in swarms;
buzzing around in my head
your whispers
bouncing off my pillow
repeating,

I love you,

I love you.

I tried to chase the shadows
thrown against the walls by
the ceiling fan; listening
to the tick of the pull chain
against the lamp
and mute; I try to
suffocate you in the silence
of make believe.

STAYING

There are times I think
the only reason we stay
and endure the pain is
because the other option
is to be alone. And although
it hurts sometimes, we still feel
something, even if it is only
two warm arms when the
world out there is so cold.

TRINKET BOX

I waited for a sun that would never shine
while the moon draped me in solace
and night kissed my lips blue.

A fading gem, locked away,
accompanying charms
in his trinket box.

Stealing air beneath a frigid bed
of October's tears. Finding truths
caked under ravaged fingernails.

Dismal reflections crept through
in a pelting rain of betrayal's footsteps
and burning lungs from holding on.

A DAY WITH THE CRAZIES

It felt like before,
secretive and misleading.
I didn't trust him,
his actions or his words,
and it was all his fault;
he shouldn't have betrayed me.

But I didn't want to spend the day
with the crazies, all of those
who what when where why and what-ifs
poisoning my mind, nauseating my belly,
and building a lump in my throat.

Talk to me, tell me,
help me understand,

and in return, he reminded me,
I am *crazy* and I
think too god damn much,
always *accusing,*
always *mad* and he
just can't take it anymore.

It's really no fun for me either,
I said.

SWEET VINDICATIONS

Rising in the background;
a storm, welling up in my chest, beating
against the outer banks of stability,
and I am sick—choking on
a tongue full of fear, burrowed in my throat while
my eyes turn gray and hazily fix on a
pitiless face, spitting sweet vindications.

And I'm left here; a ghost to wander this
shore of cracked looking glasses,
turning my back to passing ships and I . . .
I wonder if he knows . . .
I would have died for him anyway.

VERTIGO

Abstract whispers,
across forbidden lips.
Rolling thunder,
waking butterflies.

Vertigo.

Entranced in a
crippling stare
of confound perception;
deceived by
a naive heart,
enthralled
by a furtive phantom.

KEEP YOU HERE

I want to keep you here
for just a while longer
on the lobe of my ear where
your whispers replay
and on my lips
in the sweetness of wine
that lulls the pain.

I want to keep you here
for just a while longer
on this fragrant pillow
scented with you
and on the tip of my pen
that leaks your memory
and conjures you
into my dreams.

WHITE FLAG

Lay me down and
kiss away my blues;
love me until I'm dead.
The troubles in my heart
run deep and cold,
ending only by damnation.
My fight is gone
and my white flag
goes out to you;
save me with your breath
even if it's only
lies to be told.
I promise to believe.

LIVID

Those words
rolled off his tongue like honey,
leaving rose petal trails to his bed.
These tears
roll down my face in fury,
as I paint my lips livid red.

LOOK ME IN THE EYE WHEN YOU SAY GOODBYE

They barreled into my gut
like a runaway freighter
stealing my breath
gasping
as they rumbled through
like thunder in my chest

and as *why* lies dormant on
the curve of my lips
I watched his head
drop and turn away;
too cowardly to watch me die

YOU SAID NEVER

I can't get you out of my mind.
You keep playing me over and over again,
through FM stations as I drive,
and I can't help but wonder if you hear it too,
while your lying there or passing through
this side of town that you left for her
when all you ever said was never,
and yet, there you are.

THE ROAD MOST TRAMPLED

Go on—
cry now,
cry
and see
what you should have done.
Hindsight bludgeons the heart
doesn't it?
But I am numb.

Tell me
how bright lights
hypnotize,
and disguise
through influenced eyes.

And the road most trampled,
lined with lace,
is a drug on the lips
of a pretty face.
Knowing,
seeing the sign
clearly marked

Dead End,
but you still gave in.

One last drag,
exhaling stale lies
and poison
with stinging despise,

strangling trust
in foul disgust.

Watch me go,
watch me.
Because you said I couldn't,
and you thought I wouldn't,
go on,
cry now,
cry.

TRULY SORRY

I do not plea for your suffering,
an apology will pain you enough,
for you are truly sorry,
and worthless and disgusting and
oh how I laugh at and
revel in the joy of the burning of
your eyes set upon me—
me;
the one you loosed for
cowardice and whorish indulgences,
and now,
that dirty, tight, and suffocating
shell of contempt and weight of your
glare upon me as nothing;
nothing good,
nothing beautiful,
nothing worthy in your
fathers eyes,
now, filled with such remorse
looking at what I have become
without you,
and I laugh,
and I spin and dance and
frolic in ecstasy and I—
I hurt no more, while you—
you petrified little man
are left to wonder
if it's you I speak of.

DEATH TO A SALESMAN

White-washed pale sky backdrops the dark, chiseled
face of a salesman, where boastful crows sweep across
in symmetry. Chilled brushes across a starched cheek;
unable to draw even a slight form of emotion; for words,
meaningless and desensitized—scattering away—lies fly
like seeds for hungry spirits to chase in winter wind,
and believing goes out the window in a gusty yawn.

LEFTOVER RAINDROPS

you are now
only leftover raindrops
falling from weathered trees
that canopy dark and gloomy streets
and occasionally plop on the windshield—
I remember . . .
then wipe you away

JAGGED LITTLE PIECES
~PIECES OF DEPRESSION~

RAGE

Maybe one day
I will wake to realize
that not even rivers can run away
from what is supposed to be.

And they, too, rage when it storms.

DON'T BOTHER

Don't bother,
I'll hurt myself
more than you ever could.
Drop your weapons,
your words and stones
I can break myself
with a bottle and pen.
Give me a minute
alone with my sins,
no need to push,
I'll jump in.
I'll hurt myself
more than you ever could,

so don't bother.

HOME SICK

My body is sickened by
stark moments of living that
I know not how to practice,
and notes of musky fragrance;
old, worn out memories,
bitter in my mouth.
Pale skin hidden from sun,
darkened only by shadows
and night behind drawn drapes.
Leaking nauseated whimpers
that no one wants to hear, from
a hole in the mattress where
death will find me alone,
hands submerged in faded keys
of insufferable divulgence.

IT'S NOT ALWAYS GOOD TO BE HONEST

It's not easy to write of oneself
and be honest; completely honest,
to strip naked in words that burst from
filthy fingers on a once thieving hand
that lies on a sucker for believing.
Fingers that always point away, towards
Mother usually, and one upright for God.
Secrets spoiled, that this person is
fucking mad; mad at the world
avoiding every reality, to wander in a
world of make believe give a damn,
existing in a memory-saturated loaf of a
tormented mind. And these same fingers,
plunging the throat deep, gagging and puking
for someone else's dreams. And the only truth
to shed its cowardly cloak speaks up to say,
It's not always good to be honest.

IT'S CALLED I DON'T KNOW

It hurts: living, breathing—being.
All of it hurts and there are no answers
because the question is just as elusive.
Don't ask me *why* when I don't know myself.
Don't tell me how to feel better unless
you can tell me how bad I feel.
It—whatever *it* is—has swallowed me and
I lie here in the pit of its cold, dark stomach
being eaten alive by its bile and I—
I don't even know if I want to be saved.

SPRING IS STILL FOREVER AWAY

Death and heartbreak have taken my soul,
leaving me stripped and naked like
skeleton trees of winter,
frail and tortured by the cold.
And I stand shaking,
limbs writhing in razor winds
whipping and tearing me apart.
I cannot run from the reaper's hand
as he thrives on my tears,
rooting me to memories of agonies
and all I can do is stand and watch
as they hang over my head,
replaying in a dismal sky,
piercing me with his frigid sting,
electrocuting any sense of happiness
that tries to emerge.
And spring is still forever away.

RED WINE AND NORAH JONES

soft—
the caress of piano keys
and a breathy, soprano serenade
heavy, my lids become, then fall
under her spell and
lost to dream of
smoke filled bars, or open fields
licking sweet red from my lips
watching the candle, dancing
and the world
no longer exists here, in this
worry and woe burdened reality
it doesn't exist
I tell myself
as long as the music keeps playing
and the cigarette doesn't burn out
I want to stay here
numb

ENDLESS FALL INTO EBONY SANDS

Sweeping thoughts,
a soft tickle across ivory keys.
Melancholy is my soul,
my heart cumbersome.
Solitary notes of hollow ire
penciled in.
Left to myself in what seems to be
an endless fall into ebony sands.

Echoed notions steeped in dismay
reverberate as my companions,
seeking refuge in tears
and resounding chords of self-pity.
Though, in time,
when once again the music plays,
these matters; superficial
will be nothing of affect.
An embarrassment, a reminder,
a lesson perhaps;
to make me stronger,
or so they say.

ANXIETY AND MENTHOLS

there is some joy in the struggle
I suppose
fighting with myself all the way to nowhere
twiddling fingers, flicking ash from menthols
waiting for parting clouds in a florescent lamp
while my heart races and rages
waiting
waiting
waiting
and my lips become raw
from pulling skin between my teeth
my lungs holding onto air
like handlebars in a downhill run
and I can't see the bottom
for the sting to my eyes
and the screaming in my ears
a million answers rolling in a drum
and I lean in; an onward pursuit
ready for the crash that will spill them

FALLING DOWN

Sometimes I think maybe
being sad is better than being dead,
maybe, just maybe pain and feeling,
feeling something, even if it hurts,
is better than nothing at all.
Maybe, holding on is better than letting go
and holding on will keep me from being sad.
And so it becomes a mental game of
Ring Around the Rosie just to end up
that I'm the only one falling down, or maybe,
maybe I am crazy like they all say and I should
just confess, since that seems to be the
first step of approval. But, either way, I lose
and they win, again.

DON'T NOTICE ME

You're surrounded by
people and voices and noises,
but there you are,
alone; trembling inside
and you want to be invisible.
Please,
don't notice me.
Curled up inside yourself,
fearing that soon,
someone will acknowledge you
and
you will have to speak,
you will have to smile,
you will have to
convince them that
you are normal and you
try to hide from their eyes.
Please,
don't notice me.
And you wring your hands,
or shake your leg,
or bite your lip,
holding your breath,
silently pleading,
Please,
don't notice me.

SLEEPING BEAUTY

This skin is a tomb
with a million locks and
no keys to free me.
Comatose, I lie gasping
for a breath of desire.
Visitors at my graveside,
mourning what used to be of me,
with only petal offerings
and no divine flowers
of answers.
The key, they say,
is inside.

Wake up. Wake up. Wake up.

HERE AGAIN

I'm here again,
lost in this agonizing gulley,
fighting demons with
scorched eyes and dying inside;
faced with emerging thoughts from
dead conversations that slither in my head.
Back in this hole, this dark tunnel of
endless reels playing back words and
lies and moments that first led me here,
here again; sick,
questioning motives and analyzing
every single word and look they gave me
while I hide behind a smile,
gritting my teeth and trying to picture my own face
and how it must look to them,
wondering what is it that I can't see that is
so clear in their eyes and it drives me here again,
to fight insecurities and self-doubt,
screaming inside but they only see
a painted shell of an awkward girl just
wanting approval that they will never give,
so I'm here again, shaking
and pushing everyone back so they can't
see inside this place that buries me
where I wait for their gavels to stop falling.

LURKING BENEATH THE SURFACE

I've never known for certain what lie ahead, but fear's persistence
seems to lurk beneath the surface of fake smiles and wasted tears,
both conjured in vain for things, and people, who will not matter in
the end. I think about my day of mourning, when they, too, will
swallow tears of the same, sharing stories of good days gone by,
leaving out those bitter words and bruises they inflicted;
all to tell tales of happiness for their own selfish comfort.

Though I suffer, I dare not give pleasure to ears of those who
take joy in my misery. Instead, I'll just smile and let them believe;
conclusions drawn on what I allow them to see, far from the
truth of a tortured heart who only ever wanted love; the same kind of love
that I've given, completely and wholly and without reservation only to be
left unnoticed, once again, leaving another scar, another bitter bone and
one more reason to add another brick to my shelter of scattered reasoning.

I've never claimed perfection; I know my flaws and knew them well.
How could I? Mother would not let me forget; I am the other daughter.
She could always be counted on to pour salt into wounds and
diagnose the sickness that keeps everyone fevered; oblivious to the fact that
the illness is hereditary, or maybe she's just in denial. Either way,
Mother's finger was always stiffly aimed at someone other than herself.

I always expect to be the target. A victim I know well,
locking myself inside my blue walls with no windows, waiting to die,
only to endure a spiritual death instead. But, to confess my woes would
lead to recovery, and recovery . . . to happiness.
And finding happiness to me, would be like boarding a plane to a
foreign country, alone, not speaking a word of the language and that thought,
once again, brings back the fear that lies lurking beneath the surface.

IN MY HEAD

I say, *if I tell you how I feel*
you'll think I'm crazy.
There's a place inside me
that keeps pulling me in
and I don't like going there.

Sometimes,
it makes me sad,
it shows me things about myself
that I don't want to see,
but I believe them
and I cry.

Sometimes,
it makes me angry,
it tells me things that
I don't want to hear and
I think they're lies,
but I believe them
and I scream.

And sometimes,
it makes me scared,
it locks the door and
turns off the lights
and all I see are
skeletons I want to forget,
and I shut down.
But, they say
it's all in my head.

WAITING OUT THE RAIN

Sheer, veiled curtains hang
on a window to a life outside,
draping my face from prying eyes,
my hand against the cold glass,
watching clouds drift by
like my days here
in a dying soul's bed,
waiting out the rain,
listening to thunder
rolling around in my head,
waiting out the rain
in a dying soul's bed.

WHO'S LAUGHING NOW

Names buried in my chest,
because I ate my feelings.
They laughed and snickered,
especially her,
with their made up songs
and pointed fingers.
So, I ate some more,
hiding myself away
with only a pen
and an old notebook.
Who's laughing now?

MIRROR, MIRROR

I stared into the mirror today
and for a moment I saw beauty
in that girl looking back at me.
I asked where she had been
and why she kept herself hidden.

And I thought of happiness;
how I want to leave smiling,
and leave smiles on others
when they think of me.

I looked at myself,
on the inside and out and
saw only angry deception
and how it keeps its hand
tightly over my mouth, and

it has done so for so long
that the girl who used to be
is a stranger on my ear,
and now, in the mirror, because

the food tasted better than
the alcohol,

her eyes became full with pity,
feeling sorry for herself
as I always seem to do,
and once more she disappeared

inside a large shell of insecurity,
locked away again, silently screaming,
and I placed a pillow over my face
and cried out with her.

TANTRUM

It swells then crashes down
on top of anyone and anything
lying in its path, and burns and
turns to ash inside a hollow chest
where blood boils and rushes
and beats and throbs in her head,
and seeps from her clenched palms.
A biting tongue un-clamped, writhes
and lashes like a whip into flesh,
ripping and shredding without
remorse for tears, asking why,
for eyes that plea for the calm and
beg understanding for the madness
unleashed from a face that was
a clear blue sky just moments before,
but now rages like a beast set free,
seeking revenge on the one who
caged her. And they scream
and claw and battle her demons
until she falls tired and sleeps,
only then does mercy come
when she locks herself down,
crashing onto her bed of regret
and hides her face of shame.

POOR ME

This goddamn lump is back,
it hurts, but I still fight it;
maybe the smoke will burn it out
now, that's better.
Just forget it already,
this is not the first time
and probably won't be the last,
but I just can't
let
go.
Loneliness scares me,
damn, how can I even speak those words?
What a failure I've become to myself.
Who the fuck is this person?
What have I done with me?
Poor me,
poor me.
My god, just listen to this shit,
whining about things I can fix.
God, grant me the serenity
or the courage to pull the trigger.

SILENT HOLLOWS

I run away but
I'm still right there
inside the hollows of
devilish whispers and stares,
running away.

In closed up spaces
behind locked doors,
alone with silent walls,
I still hear the noise
in silent walls.

I run away, but
I'm still right there
in silent hollows,
running away.

JAGGED LITTLE PIECES

Chaos in fists full of hair, left behind from
train wrecks that I have caused,
devouring remains of anything clinging,
but for a minute, normalcy fakes a smile,
in which you place too much hope.

It won't be long before I'm bitch-slapped by crazy
and I become jagged little pieces, shattered and
scattered from a place I'm not willing to visit,
yet.

And because of this, you should get off the tracks.

I'm sorry your glue doesn't stick. I'm sorry you love me.

AFTERSHOCK

There blows that train again,
dragging its feet and moping
long, sobbing cries resounding
through this dreary place where
time has ceased to move onward,
and it echoes my sorrow with its
grieving moan, howling inside my
empty chest, ricocheting off my
decaying walls where ghosts have
chiseled and scratched at the
lining, leaving only holes and
fragments of what used to be, in
scattered, shattered remnants,
lying, dying in the hollows of this
stagnant soul and its rumbling sobs,
shake off the decay of dust and ash,
where I crumble in its aftershock.

SEA OF ABANDON

inside repute words
I fall helpless
stirring a sea of abandon

ebbing into the depths
of deep blues
resist
swept mercilessly under
and gravity clenches

tenacity wanes
peeling away inhibitions
one
by
one

swallow me

THE DOLOR OF STANDING STILL

I feel

d i s c o n n e c t e d

and the world is not waiting for me.

I watch life

       passing

through gaps in curtain sheets,

and time keeps

f

a

l

l

i

n

g

smoldering at my feet.

.

SOME TIME

I keep telling myself
it's not just me,
everybody is sad sometimes,
sometimes,
but sometimes has become
some time for me, gone in
irreplaceable minutes,
swallowed by a timeless clock
holding my life in its
steady moving hands,
unstoppable and unwilling
to wait for me to smile
while the world taunts me
with echoing laughter.

WICKED LITTLE THINGS

Much like the burn of
an aged, dark liquor,
there will be pleasure from the pain,
and I drink it like a dying weed,
remorseless
because my thirst for the rise
overpowers that little voice
sitting on my right shoulder.

And guilt only comes
when consequence meets reality
and I am forced
to confront the demons I birthed
from lying down with sin.

THEY CALL IT THE BLUES

Stroking fingers
down her long neck,
she moans
a beautiful orgasmic mewl,
vibrating inside me
through a thick mist
of amber-tinted smoke.
I listen; engrossed
with a bourbon-drenched heart.

Swaying, swaying
meditative hums
as if his hands were on me.
Closing my eyes allowing her cry
to infuse my body
with her emollient whine.

Speaking to me of memories.

Intoxicated
in melodious ecstasy,
and I wonder why
they call it the blues.

SKIES OF PEACH CHARDONNAY

Skies of peach Chardonnay—
the memories flood my mind;
with seeping eyes I drift away.

Plummeting heart strangles my throat,
as tears streak through lonely notes.

Fingertips softly tracing red velvet;
a timeless trance
sweeps me from my element.

Gloomy grays smolder the landscape,
smothering reality and I cannot escape.

For in this moment, I submit to the pain
while the skies drink of peach Chardonnay.

OF WHICH PIECE TO FALL

Dangling from this
cliff of rectification,
I cling to the hand of me.
Be her god and save her,
or let her fall away.
But, of which do I let go?
Whose death will
profit the other?
Or, will death be the
vantage of the dying.

ROAMING BETWEEN SHORES
~PIECES OF HOPE~

REBORN

Creation;
earth seed inside
the womb of God
encapsulated in Love.
Unborn; floating in waiting
to be birthed into
a world we only dream.
A world imagined; fabricated images.
And we are not yet born
until we shed our cocoon of flesh,
we have not yet lived until the soul
takes its first breath of death,
inhaling stardust.
And fear will become understanding;
foreign prophecies, finally
deciphered.

THE DOOR IS LOCKED TO NEVERLAND

I find myself wondering if time and God are real.
If one day time will cease and God will touch my fingertips
and this will all make sense. I wonder if I have done
what I was placed here to do or if that, too, is just make-believe.
I read in the good book that we must all come as children.
Does that mean we should have the imagination of a child
in order to see heaven?

I wonder.

Do we pour our hearts into this fairy tale of
golden streets and angel wings to only be chewed up and
spat out by the tiny tooth still lying beneath our pillow?
Faith. Have *faith.*
I breathe and ponder some more as that word dies in my head.
Life and the people in it, what we surround ourselves in,
the spirits we allow to embrace our world and influence our
little, spongy brain: does that create more than company for a time?
In the end, will they have created our eternity by squeezing out
a splattered vision from absorbed moments we shared,
leaving the canvas dark as hell's midnight, or will we
wade in happy yellow streams like fearless children,
behind pearl gates that keep out the demons?

Think happy thoughts
and dream your life away and you may get your wings.
Or else your soul is damned, because you were afraid to believe.
How fair is that when all you know, is how to feel bad?
When all the fairy tales locked their door on you and
every friend wore an angry hat?
How do you close your eyes and not be afraid?

WHAT HOPE FEELS LIKE

It feels like those little towns;
those miniature, ceramic houses
and churches sitting on mantles
and beneath the tree at Christmas,
softly lit with white lights;
a melancholy glow
that warms you with nostalgia,
but feels sad at the same time;
sitting there on fluffy, fake snow
sprinkled with glitter,
shining
on the outside,
empty
on the inside, but still waiting
for something magical to happen.

SADNESS WEARS A HALO

It hangs above me like
a streetlamp in the night,
not yet enough to light the
dour of darkness, but pressing
with a salving glow
through the drape of fear
of things beneath
a halo of persuasion that
I might again see the day
and survive the demons
hiding in the shadows.

SHOOTING PAINS

My hand hurt—
shooting pains.
I made a fist,
then let go,
squeezing repeatedly to
make it go away, but
it kept reminding me
of the gun
and how heavy it was
in my hand,
before I decided
I would lay it back down
and try again.

CURIOSITIES OF THE MOON

Peeking from a sullen cloak,
a wondering eye.
If I give myself to you
what will you do differently,
asked tomorrow of today,
with prodding curiosity.

Will you thank me and
be grateful or
do you make un-kept promises
to another sun?
What do you want,
the past is dead and
you mourn with regrets.

Will you continue to
look back on my grave in sorrow
as you name me *yesterday*
and beg my brother for
one more day,
or will you hold me
like I am
the only one left.

SILENT RIVERS

In a jungle of noise I seek a silent river
to wash away the pain and regrets
from my blood-soaked hands and she
hides from me, like an angel in waiting,
until I stop trying to understand.

And when I reach the edge of despair
she shows herself, revealing truths louder
than the rumbling lies inside my head.

ROAMING BETWEEN SHORES

like the shadow
cast from the shade tree
slow moving like the day
or the leaf,
fell upon the river and
carried in wafted breeze,
away and alone
drifting to where the current leads
I, the tree—
my heart, the shadow
and the leaf—my spirit,
slow moving like the day

CARRYING BAGS

It's a rolling highway,
one we all travel, carrying bags
filled with tears, dreams, the past;
with collected things from the road behind,
and we're looking to barter.

But our souls are very different;
some have holes, while others
have just begun to wear.

And we all take this journey,
bags in hand,
hoping someone will offer a map,
wise and wrinkled,
and we all are just looking
for the same thing.

HIDING IN THE LOST AND FOUND

Sometimes, the only way to ever find yourself
is to get completely lost,
so bent,
so broken,
so shattered that . . .
the only words you can find are
I. give. up.
And at that moment of release, of
letting go of everything and everyone and
all the little, fragile, meaningless parts
holding you together; that shell of
fear and inhibitions will begin to fall
piece by piece, lie by lie,
until all that remains is flesh,
bare, naked, honest flesh, unveiled and
free and weightless and
illuminated by the light of truth
and washed in the rain of pure clarity,
and you find yourself overwhelmingly present
with an urgency to live.

CATCHING A BREATH OF HOPE

There's a whole world out there, full of
people feeling the same way; hurting,
loving, laughing, screaming,
inside,
outside.
All the same but separated by circumstances that
tell them, you do not belong here. You are not
like me. You are different.
And mirrors tell the same lies, with so much value
given to this breakable glass of distorted illusions.
And people die, they die every day,
inside,
outside.
And more and more people are clinging to pain,
embracing the hurt because its burn is the
only warmth they know, while they plea silently
in coded words and type them onto a screen, and
hide in caves beneath the covers because
facing the world means smiling, and how can they
smile when life is bearing down on their chest, squeezing
out dreams into cages where existing becomes only

inhale,

exhale,

and catching a breath of hope is
nearly impossible, but we keep going.

ONE LONE BIRD

One lone bird on a wire
pondering his direction
watching dawn break
and christen the sky
spilling morning in peach sun drops
onto storefront windows and into
those once darkened corners of night
pushing shadows around the yellowing maples
and as a chilled breeze lifts and
swirls the leaves in the street
he spreads his wings and flies
disappearing into the rays
leaving behind the cold
in search of warmer days

WISHFUL CLEANSING

I hope and wish and dream and pray
that I will someday find my way
I miss the girl who used to be
A heart that built no boundaries

When worry hid in unknown places
and all the world was friendly faces
Oh the innocence time erases
what bitter creatures life can make us

If only I could take a minute
remember youth and get lost in it
I'd bathe my soul inside that moment
and forget the world is my opponent

I'd give back all I've learned through years
and all the days I've seen through tears
I'd release these bonds of blinding grief
and find the girl inside of me

Set free the dove of peace and rest
to lift this anchor off my chest
and finally recognize my place
in a world of amazing grace

LET GO

Morning breaks in the distance
and that low hanging fog crawls away;
rebirth and redemption for
all sorrow-filled things
lighting softly a new direction
for those willing to see.

And yesterday is swallowed
by a beautiful horizon
as she sings a song through all the earth
for the memory of weeping,
let go, let go,
for all now is pardoned.

MY OWN

I am my own
light in the darkness of a selfish world,
the sun of my winter, my shelter, my warmth

I am my own
mother as I nurture my body and soul,
love unconditional; discipline for growth

I am my own
friend to save me from bullets and tears,
forsaking me never in pressure of peers

I am my own
hero in battles defending myself,
counting last upon others and first on myself

LESSONS

I have managed to fly
with broken wings,
and I learned the force against me
can be used to push me farther

I have stood back up
after being shoved down,
and I learned that being on the bottom
brings appreciation at the top

I have been confronted
for wrongs I have made,
and I learned that owning up
builds courage and re-builds respect

I have been broken
into a million tiny pieces,
and I learned to be thoughtful
in how they're placed back together

I have suffered
through chaos and death,
and I learned to fight
to make every moment happy

I have lived
not a lifetime, nor a short time,
but I have learned
to survive the imperfections of life

SURRENDER HEART

mute the thunder of a shattered vessel
and desiccate its purloined hull of bitter waters
so she may concede quietly into deep resolution,
yield not to him sobering winds and harbor the watcher
who has shown his lamp for the newly christened,
yet boast fiercely of solitary winds and ill skies in
weeping rage for the fallen tide, who now rests
beneath your blanket of blue

WHEREVER YOU WISH TO GO

Upon the threshold of tomorrow
I linger back, unsettled.
Where will this sun lead me,
I question.

And I hear a whisper that softly says,
wherever you wish to go.

And without further reservation
I dip a toe
into the waters of tomorrow,
fearlessly content.

HAPPINESS HAIKU

Happiness flutters;
an elusive butterfly
caught between fingers

SHINE ETERNAL

Go about yourself with elated pride,
with a fearless stride, as if
the world owes you its applause.
Chin up and eyes forward, march now
to the sound of your own beating drum;
a heart that no man can, nor will,
bring rain upon, because you—
you own the sun.
Go on, shine now,
shine—
Shine eternal.

ABOUT THE AUTHOR

Kellie Elmore is a writer who believes self-expression is most beautiful in its pure, raw and unedited form, transforming the simplest words into something you can feel. Kellie finds inspiration in nature and in the humble surroundings of her "backyard"—Southeast Tennessee. Through her charming prose and engrossing narratives, Kellie writes freely on many subjects both fiction and semi-autobiographical, penning her way through cherished and magical moments as well as tragic losses. Her goal is to take readers back, rekindle a memory, or elicit a feeling.

Follow Kellie:
Website: kellieelmore.com
Twitter: @Kellie_Elmore
Facebook: facebook.com/magicinthebackyard

www.ingramcontent.com/pod-product-compliance
Lightning Source LLC
Chambersburg PA
CBHW070812050426
42452CB00011B/2009